FROM THE VIRGIL CAVERNS

BY THE SAME AUTHOR

FROM THE
VIRGIL CAVERNS

Peter Redgrove

CAPE POETRY

Published by Jonathan Cape 2002

2 4 6 8 10 9 7 5 3 1

First published in Great Britain in 2002 by
Jonathan Cape
Random House, 20 Vauxhall Bridge Road,
London SW1V 2SA

Random House Australia (Pty) Limited
20 Alfred Street, Milsons Point, Sydney,
New South Wales 2061, Australia

Random House New Zealand Limited
18 Poland Road, Glenfield,
Auckland 10, New Zealand

Random House South Africa (Pty) Limited
Endulini, 5A Jubilee Road, Parktown 2193, South Africa

The Random House Group Limited Reg. No. 954009
www.randomhouse.co.uk

A CIP catalogue record for this book
is available from the British Library

ISBN 0-224-06236-0

Papers used by Random House are natural,
recyclable products made from wood grown in sustainable forests;
the manufacturing processes conform to the environmental
regulations of the country of origin

Typeset by Palimpsest Book Production Limited,
Polmont, Stirlingshire
Printed and bound in Great Britain by
Biddles Ltd, Guildford and King's Lynn

to the Falmouth companions
in poetry who saw us through

CONTENTS

ACKNOWLEDGEMENTS

Acknowledgements are due to the editors of the following:

Acumen, *Agenda*, *Ambit*, *Boomerang*, *Haiku Quarterly*, *Interpreter's House*, *Ixion*, *London Magazine*, *Manhattan Review*, *Poetry Ireland*, *Poetry London*, *Poetry Review*, *Poetry Wales*, *Poet's Voice*, *Psychopoetica*, *Stride*, *Swansea Review*, *Sulfur*, *The Shop*, *Thumbscrew*, *The Times Literary Supplement*

'Circus Wheel' was commissioned for the anthology of the 1999 Salisbury Festival, *Last Words* (Picador, 1999)

The author gratefully acknowledges the financial assistance of The Authors' Foundation.

ARRIVALS

The spider in her draughty great halls
            hanging by her fists
                        from the rafters,
A few dried leathers
            and wings like cracked windshields
                        dangling from the radii;
Harley Davidson chassis without engines
            hollow as bongoes;
                        washing machine in energetic renewal,
Revision, a cube of hasty
            hurricane water hurrying,
                        a tornado shaking
In my father's scullery
            wearing white like his doctor
                        whose white coats
Have to be washed somewhere,
            bring him close to the ghost
                        every rotation a whiteness;
My father turning up at Paddington
            in his car, for a surprise,
                        smiling at his fingertips
Like a conjurer with his four-wheel cabinet
            laughing at his traffic adroitness
                        like a conjurer
Producing himself from the shiny coachwork;
            today he lost the way:
                        all the streets wept
So well known to him;
            his knowledge went,
                        his engine stopped,
Emptied. I know
            how it was,
                        he showed me something else

That belonged to both of us
with the engines stopped
and the halls draughty,
Close to the ghost;
his knowledge went, and mine followed,
catch it before
It leaves like a ghost,
on these stepped verses;
on these stairs met together,
These radii.

AT THE OLD POWERHOUSE

(Kingston on Thames)

A swan stretching
            its neck like a javelin speeds
                        a couple of metres
Above the roughened river,
            the stridor of its breath-shaped
                        wings like the creaking
Of a supple switch, a whipstock;
            descending further, the swan steps
                        across the water in five
Giant strides, in five
            mighty braking steps, settles
                        its own foldings
Among the waterfoldings, tucks
            its wings into its armpits, shrugging
                        them in, and yachts onward
As a serenely-sailing ornamental waterbird
            reborn out of the turbulent and draughty
                        air-voyager;
The river glitters like errant electricity
            and a watermusic floats downstream,
                        a jazz funeral no less
With a band and a catafalque and a small black barge
            full of golden instruments;
                        the powerhouse draws itself up
To attention like the old soldier
            it is; I expect smoke from the broken
                        chimneys, from the colossal
Hearth-chambers, but those
            are swifts coiling on the air
                        as the music coils

In the air that rushes
              sonorously through
                              the river-doubled
Trumpets and trombones.

THE WEEPING BAR

The bamboo hide is for
   bird-watching over the lake
     there is a bar to lean on
To weep on; the lake won't mind, nor the birds
   that write large whispers over it,
     for watching and weeping,
To watch the water settle
   its mirrors, then spun
     by the wind making
The invisible visible,
   or revolved by the ducks paddling
     immense cogs and mainsprings
Time-telling on the water.
   In the hideout
     it is dry and dusty,
A little girl settles down
   to weep next to me leaning
     on the bar, the pole
Like a dancer's barre, she staring
   out over the lake, watching through
     the flowing water
Of her eyes at the circling water;
   the hut fills up
     with people who have come
To watch, and to weep, same thing,
   or close enough.

CIRCUS WHEEL

(vertical and horizontal)

I

They have driven the Ferris
                out on to the hill
                                powered it with
Its own generators fetched
                out of the tailgate
                                of its painted lorry –
It is like a Christmas tree which
                is a round staircase
                                up to the stars
The planets and their maelstroms
                and among them swing
                                benches for the paying customers
The great wheel declares
                the fair is here
                                And at its foot kiosks cluster
Stuffed with light:
                the fortune-teller's hovel where
                                you put your life-lines
Into her palmist-hands,
                and the dodgems with their
                                high electrical tails
Sparking like meteor-swarms
                hissing on the wire-netting ceiling;
                                all raised up on the muddy green,
Hammered together in one day and one
                night, it is a piece of
                                star-sky come down

On to the hill and full
                of folk in this one day
                                the hinge in the year
Where one may peruse
                star-machinery in close-up
                                raised up on 28 benches
Viewing the mysteries,
                hanging on the wheel,
                                as in the grand circular tent
Or marquee
                or tabernacle the horses wheel, gallop
                                each with its mistress
Standing tall
                and smeared with sequins
                                like glittering
Stallion-stuff.

II

The Wheels of the Fair,
                the outer
                                and the inner as fair,
The outer, the Fairies' Wheel
                in which the 28 moon-benches
                                climb to their height
Pulling the reins
                of the earth's water
                                like a round harp
And like this equestrienne
                wearing her khaki
                                rehearsal-shirt
The colour of earth
                riding the circus-ring
                                like a cavalry

She is called Ms O
           horsed, the ring is her route,
                like a Centauress
With mountainous
          horse-thews
              she traces out that
Deep castle of hers,
        with the dewy pond:
              the spinning castle of horseback
And its water is the same
        glittering stuff
           as the estuary water in which
The lights revolve
        that circus which must descend
           so fair it is,
The Mare-Mother's ring
        the woman's
              circular fountain,
She rides
        the fairest thing.

RESIN

His Walkman speaking into him
    two bees tugging and squeaking
      at the flowers of his ears
The shoals of herring
    the schools of whales that pull
      across the harbour water
In oily sperm
    in rainbows of it and clotted butterpats;
      dews of the women,
Resins of them:
    it was the gardening
      she had not yet done
But planned to do before tea, perfumed her
    as the weather does –
      flowers alter time;
A man cycling, carrying daffodils
    in the crook of his arm.
      the flowers
Like see-through sails
    fan out their scent
      as he pedals emitting
A full-rigged ghostyacht
    in a squall of scent
      changing the scale of events,
Reaching on the port tack,
    shivering and reaching, steered
      by Walkman.

ADAGIO

How we were tortured in hell
        by I suppose we must call them
                demons, though they were
So lovely to look at and smelt so nice;
        like the bees of death
                shaking their flowers,
The ravens tearing death into strips
        on the battlefield;
                squeezing my comfortable
Sponge in the soapy bath:
        all the sounds of rebirth,
                heaven thundering in the mountain,
The squeaky cap, the shining gluten,
        the panting, the yell;
                the lichen bridesmaids
That are all skirt, the gravestones
        brided with the snow,
                beyond, a shady hall
Made of all
        the Cornish granites
                dazzlingly.dark;
The young father is staring at me –
        he is on his way
                to meet all the children
He has ever loved; the broad river
        presses foam
                under the low stone arches;
Clothes you
        can swim away in,
                dowsing clothes
With no ties;
        there's a grotto here,
                underground, but it

Slips about under the outstretched
              willows of the
                        dowsers sent to find it.

WATCHING THE VENTIFACTS

The smooth grooves
              and flutings of ventifacts,
                          the water slate dark,
The wind blows off the water
              with its verb:
                          stand up, kneel down, open this,
Look at that; what the wind says
              to do, must be done.
                          We were sealed in
Because the wind
              could not shake the storms
                          out of the huge cloudbanks:
Then it did, and the whole world poured
              in black masses
                        like the entrails
Of coalmines streaked with all minerals;
              weather that puts you in a trance
                        with its smooth-gliding
Coal-black machinery
              then plucks you out of it
                        with a relenting breeze –
Can listen to a breeze talking
              for hours moving about
                        like another person in the house
Opening and shutting doors;
              then more clouds sail
                        out of the promontory
And carry me away, or leave me
              looking up into the sky, where I can watch
The planet breathing.

MEMENTOES

(by the old powerhouse, Kingston)

I

My first line of poetry
          swam up from the river here:
                    'Rolling habitat of such
White ghosts as
          cold Ophelia . . .'; she
                    who must be obeyed, she
Who is wet
          swam into my dreams,
                    singing among her
Red wet flowers.

II

Villas of enormous wealth
          line the river-banks, great
                    house-cage menageries
Brilliantly lighted and brilliantly reflected:
          it is like a river flowing
                    between the cages
Of lions.

III

One of those big ducks which are
          dusky cygnets has got one wing
                    hitched up, like a child

Wanting to go,
        on a clew of angler's nylon yarn,
                cannot leave cannot fly –
Can look over its shoulder at me
        defiant as a Duke tilting
                his neb among the empty
Glitter of the ballroom river
        as if to say
                'None may hinder or wet me'

IV

The Riverside Café by the old powerhouse
        heartbrokenly broken down,
                the balustrades softening
Like spongecake fingers,
        the river flowing like cold tea;
                three dressed like cardinals
Have offered to take tea
        here for powerhouse charity:
                save the monumental dynamos!
And to speak from the decayed veranda
        as hustings, eating
                and expounding how
To save the electrical house
        and refurbish it as a cathedral.
                The rain falls clothing
The cardinals in more eminent colours
        and softens the light
                as if for prayer
And spreads its puddles, within each
        a splash of personal scarlet.
                There is no roof,

Their Eminences are scarlet-wet,
                    they bite into their
                                        coldwater teacakes
The Teacake Mass, the Requiem of Scone,
                    their habits like blood
                                        with wet lights in it
Like torches approaching.
                    This ambitious prayer
                                        has not saved the old powerhouse,
Whose shadow is this avenue
                    of raining trees; not even
                                        the power of scarlet,
Of furnaces approaching.

                              v

Lingering by the sequence
                    of absent dynamos
                                        now mid-spring gardens
The child points
                    at the dragonflies
                                        hovering in twos
Bent into bows
                    electrical-blue and shuddering,
                                        shuddering and hovering;
In the walled garden
                    that was the generator hall
                                        of wheels and grease
Cables and vibration
                    shouting its RPMs,
                                        how delicate a deep
But airy flower seems to her;
                    the river flowers past
                                        carrying on its back

Myriads of white blossoms
        like Chinese teacups;
                the river, the everlasting
Powerhouse
       is stained
            to China with pollen,
And back again.

FROM THE VIRGIL CAVERNS

INTRODUCTION

'The change of perception is godlike.'

Shirokov reported
        in the *Independent on Sunday*
                (2 May 1993) on the true
Use of the cave paintings;
        the theory is that the boys
                entered the Distant Hall
Crawling on their stomachs
        through the mud
                which represented dying
Through the synaesthetic ordeal
        of the lower death-passage
                where the animals seemed
To come alive, prancing
        in the extended senses
                of the Distant Hall
Thus creating in the candidate
        his own particle
                of shared subconscious
Which they brought out unbroken
        into the world
                through the other fissure, a Yoni
A few feet higher where they are clothed
        with exterior cunt like a waterfall
                that fits them for society.

Also the stone track
> of a spiritual acrobat
>> there are clefts
And vaginal openings giving forth
> a floor of jewels
>> and many formations;
There are spires
> rising from the floor and pulling
>> from the ceilings
And often as they meet
> they meet as folded curtains
>> draped on strong bars
Or as semi-transparent screens
> pleated and folded,
>> a lamp
Shines as a rose through this alabaster.
> These bijouteries
>> in formation
In a cavern like a garage
> of old Chevrolets carved
>> in wet marble appear
In the flow of water
> covering everything,
>> appear to be rushing forward and
They are not in fact
> perfectly still since
>> like freeze-frame
They are moving through
> the millennia too slowly
>> for any movement to be seen,
Though in their stillness
> they bear about them the look

                    of racing through a mild rain-shower
Of mother o'pearl, speeding
                down pearly thoroughfares:
                            bring your lamp
To the cavern
                they are immediately present,
                            and wet, and rosy
With their presence.

The wet clock of stone
                seems stopped
                                but all the surfaces
Are moving under the water
                an inch
                                in a thousand years
The rafts of jade
                and mats of creamy alabaster
                              owned by China
And stopped under England;
                and the water-bright
                              stalactites or linghams
Slide as slowly
                downwards by the same clock
                              in the caverns
Where hollow spires
                spring up everywhere;
                              the maternal water-sculptures
Inherent in the rock
                constantly in bloom
                              from within the stone;
The caves are filling up
                with exceedingly slow
                              spires and mirrors:
The travelling church of the giants
                comes to approximate stillness
                              in this rosy rock.

So many of the walls
         depict robed guides:
                  figures painted in ores
And looming through the ever-wet
         walls; shining statues
                  upon whose heads
The waterfalls plash.
         For the humans
                  whose smoky lamps paint
Their ceilings in sfumage
         there are swifter guides,
                  Wills-of-the-wisp
Skimming the surface of the
         underground lake
                  guide the penetrant oars
And there is slow lightning
         pointing the arches, electricity
                  from the dunes
Rolling overhead . . .
         there is an echo
                  like rubberlined doors
Squashily opening and closing, for
         there is a ceremony
                  hiding round every corner;
And there are pillars of limestone
         whose table-top is hollow
                  and contains
A serving of mud; collected for centuries,
         small altars of mud
                  so heavy it is pure; everything

Here weighs heavy with purity; the sand
            underfoot drifts heavy
                        because it is so pure,
Washed and rewashed
            in the constant distillation
                        of the cavern waters;
The air is heavier here
            because of purity, and the great
                        striding arches
Are pure in form because water
            has worn them that way.
                        Close to these pedestals
In the presence of offered mud
            the walls are more nearly
                        transparent, and the guiding figures
Have approached nearer the surface,
            nearer to stepping forward
                        through the stone,
About to show their faces,
            wiping away the limestone crusts,
                        like rubbing sleepy-sand away
With the backs of their pebbled fists;
                        a virgil has burst
Through the rock-grain with its scents and lotions;
            whomsoever it is, a presence
                        passing through the Virgil Caves,
Passing through all the perfumes of Rock.

The hills hollow and chiming
   like bells
      to the gigantic labours
Of water building
   its limestone cathedral,
      excavating bells
From their native rock;
   the notes of them
      fitting each to each,
In their millions the first congregation;
   the city of stone and water
      creating itself
And telling us all about it
   from larynxes larger than
      terrene cathedrals
And from tabernacles reaching
   round the world
      where milliards sing
With each shower and gather
   into subterranean waters;
      and larynxes small
As holed pebbles
   lined with crystals
      like radio sets
Broadcast the cavern look
   to lie
      on hills that are
Caverns inside, small enough
   to take home (you could not
      take the hills home),

And listen to them there
                    natural trannies
                                    tuned to the water-stations
Or right down to the dust
                    that is dancing
                                    to mountain vibration;
And the dust
                    of the great bass explosions
                                    in slate quarries whose air
Is full of stone
                    broadcasting. The face
                                    of this climber
Is streaming
                    with creative water
                                    as he swings himself down
Through the roof's point
                    into the great hall
                                    via the shakehole or doline
The water falling over him
                    like an armour of glass
                                    his faded boilersuit charged
Shining and new
                    as dew is, ringing its bell.
                                    Above us, on the exterior slopes,
Beyond the rock-roofs
                    these woods are thickly
                                    stocked with stout pigs.

FIELD DAY

They had put him at table
        with a one-eyed man; offended
                he stalked out over the river-bridge
Past the disused forge and the Apothecary's
        dim little shop . . .
                but the field day
Had gone well,
        the geological hammers in orchestra
                chiming their rational music
Out of a science strong as the cliffs
        they studied: 'how can
                a one-eyed man make
A geologist! he cannot see
        Depth!' – abruptly he walked
                into the hanging breath
Which was the sweat of the great wood,
        and his anger
                fell away from him like garments . . .
He pointed to the study-boulder,
        granite, made of quartz,
                mica, feldspar, the unripe fruit
Of rock packed with the insect
        wings of mica, and the feldspar
                the backing for the quartz mirrors
That make the stone shine, that make
        the shadows shift inside the shine . . .
                they all took out their pocket glasses
And studied the lichens scrolling the boulder-skin, he
        asked them to observe the transformation by the
First species converting the rock they peered into
        to shallow, tall-stemmed cups of gold;
                he called it

Cladonia fimbriata with a beaming smile . . .
and secondly, the field-grey species,
Parmelia omphalodes
Rising from the centre of which
a fruiting body like a rough
clay vase, round-headed
With a slotted opening. The men murmured
at the microscopic gems evolved
to two Latin pictures
By the grey boulder out of its
greyness; geology
becomes botany without loss . . .
They fuss around for
new miracles which are everywhere
and in the rabbit-droppings
Under the magnifiers
bundles of small bales
of dry sweet herbs
Like those in the cabinet-drawers
of scented woods
of the dimly-lighted
Apothecary's shop
which is the whole wood
and middlestate
Between boulder and river . . .
he steps out into the clearing,
he shakes the one-eyed man's
Hand in warm greeting
and they are all shaking hands,
geology and geologists in one,
Subjects and objects shaking hands . . .
the wood had stepped into the shop
and nearly filled it

With its curative influences,
                lined with cabinets made of wood
                                out of sunshine and rock merging
In one great forest of herbalistic furniture.

SEA VISIT

The seagull's mew
                opens a door in the air;
                                lovemaking opens a new room
In the bedroom;
                that plump copy of *Dune*
                                simply because I bought it there
with its four hundred pages
                doors and windows, includes
                                the entire volume called Boscastle,
A door that was shut on it
                swings open,
                                a door large as the whole room,
Large as a season of the year,
                renewed in any season
                                by hearing unpredictably
That airborne throaty gull-call;
                the sea itself
                                brings its gold-irised eyes
To strut on the sill,
                its shelly beak,
                                its white and grey
Plumage of the waves:
                for the sea flies on its feathers
                                and with herring-breath
Out of the sea,
                pauses to mew,
                                opening in everything
The sea's pages.

The wings of the mirror
        in open embrace
                shaking his reflections;
The clear and happy glances of the child;
        as though he were maintained
                by her womb once more,
The son's image appears in her mirror,
        he sees himself there
                in the slightly-trembling
Panes like underground water
        he is both inside and outside the mirror
                with its powders and spraying bottles
Like creatures whose spit is perfume;
        he died while staring into
                my mother's mirror;
What mirror is not an erotic
        death-machine, especially
                a mother's:
A fresh charge of innocent dew
        to hold the image
                ready to be born,
The mirror opening, the mother's eye
        opening
                his soul carried in a single drop.

ASTRAL MACHINE

Pieces of everything
        in town sewn back together
                bound in threads of saliva
Riveted with saliva
        mortared with spit
                by the pliers of the face
The pirate-jerseyed and cutlassed
        wasps pierce their wooden
                balloon together,
In the spherical docks the wings'
        welding glare
                is an intuition machine
Whose music modulates
        with the shaping of clouds
                pitch dropping
As the clouds mass up
        they make their own thunder-buzz
                mirror of the sky
Packed with stings like lightning
        busy among their rhums
                and elixirs, their
Wasp wax and wasp honey.
        Our town overwhelms with such
                intuitional machines,
ESP machines, including
        the sea itself,
                and shells coiled for listening-
Into the sea-fetch of the air.

RESERVOIRS OF PERFECTED GHOST

(From the Virgil Caverns)

Acres of the sky having
        floated down and settled in the woods,
                the bluebell canopy spreads beneath
The green capes of the trees;
        heaven is so full of sky
                it cannot hold it – it falls
Into the woods, and spreads, heaven
        skygazing in its woodland cavern;
                bend down and pluck with admiration
A juicy stem; the blue bell
        salivates glass-juice on your fingers;
                lift this flower to your nose
It smells not at all!
        it is all of them that smells:
                the sun reaches through the leaves
And lifts the perfume out, gently
        from these masses, so as not to break it; keeping
                the shock of the blueness
As it issues from underground;
        heaven must have gone deep,
                to arrive so.

GUINIUSS

The moon sprawls
        in the choppy water but
                swims in the Guinness
Without pretext; the raft
        of the star, its reflection in stout:
                it is a land aching
For its music-map; a Guinness
        standing on the bar
                like a pint of black cat;
She exposes her tenderometer lips
        for him, raises the trombone,
                the windy shrine of breath;
The music spins out
        in travelling shells the colour
                of invisible Guinness;
While it changes its skin
        the serpent is blind; the player
                ends her riff
And changes her skin from
        trombone to sax; your actual glass
                is half-empty with dark
As you drink it; swallows
        of silence travel the bar's length
                while simultaneously all
Drink, closing their eyes
        while they drink to music
                which is silence as well.

PERSONAL STONES

I

Coal hung round the neck
        a jet necklace,
                anthracite hard enough
To be cut and polished
        like a gem
                warmed on the neck
And throat to give
        the smell of millennial
                forests rising,
Uttered from words
        that are god-solid.

II

A lodestone wand
        attracts thunder
                don't carry it
in your trouser-pocket,
        but it makes memory
                more retentive
As the iron ideas associate
        in ropings of the lodestone field;
                this scree is lodestone,
Clings to the nails
        in your shoes
                muffled like slippers
In fur of iron;
        near are the dunes
                of lodestone sand

Shuddering, building and rebuilding,
                        magnetising the wind
Forming topiary mazes
            from broadcasts like this
                        radio concert
From the Birmingham Symphony Orchestra
            made solid again
                        this side of transmission
For the magnetic iron shifting
            recreates radio patterns
                        in ropes of sand
And the sea's shock sends
            thunder back into the music; fat
                        sparks modulate
Its black thundercloud slopes;
            there are houses and beds
                        hewn from the living stone,
Lovingstone that keeps its power
            for ever, or do I presume,
                        Doctor Livingstone?

MY FATHER'S ROVER

Father's car
          like the groans
                   of Loch Ness
Hypnotises, his beams
          sweep across
                   the darkened ceiling,
His rhythm as
          a driver
                   hypnotises
He brushes his moustache
          with a forefinger
                   like a hypnotist;
The roads of Surrey
          are like a sounding groove
                   like the grooves
Of a gramophone,
          he plays them
                   with his car and
The road-music idles
          sleepily into the passenger
                   he hypnotises
With his car,
          hasped mesmeric box
                   inset with gems
Of brilliant cut,
          the world flows past,
                   the dark world
Flows past
          as the jewelbeams touch it
                   it is blackwhite flowing
It is the needle that
          plays the dark;
                   by the spin

Of a wheel
        he changes the programme,
                the scenery.

TSUNAMI

The tidal wave
        it rushes upon the coast
                so fast everything
Seems still, hangs for a moment
        like veined stone
                over the off-white hotels –
It speeds-in faster than tigers
        running, its body striped
                with currents and bannered
Armies of kelp, this great Crystal
        Palace toppling overhead,
                inside you can see
The boarding-houses and chapels
        twisting over and over,
                the arms of the dock-cranes
Knotting and unknotting
        inside the glossy flank;
                inscribed on the wheeling
Precipices are shining
        whirlpools deep
                but stable as if drilled,
Snaky corridors;
        he dives into one
                of these vaginas
Before the wave-head
        champs him up
                in foaming teeth,
And he is crest-carried along
        like a pilot
                in his cockpit,
Pilot of Leviathan, while she
        roars and falls
                without ceasing to fall.

He is buoyed
               in his personal maelstrom
                             and makes a safe touchdown,
Face-skidding
               on blackmirror mud
                         that is salty
And without horizon, or circumference,
               like God's Hinder Parts;
                         the hunched green wave far-off
Is still pouncing under its cape
               and shouting as it goes
                         and shuddering still
As I am shuddering.

MY FATHER'S TEETH

A bowl with my father's teeth in it
               left out in the cool moonlight
                             and the dew, cooled
Out of the night air
               in the dawn has become
                             a drink through
My father's semilunar teeth
               and world-saliva, sipped . . .
It was the same guy
               who left two phones
                             and two phone-boxes
Open on the Irish coast
               so that all he could hear in either
                             was the atmosphere
In stereo . . .

ELDERHOUSE

(Falmouth Café)

Elderly and most
        dignified in her whitesugar
                coat, rinsing the plain
China cups for the dishwasher,
        I requested tapwater
                in an ordinary tumbler
And this started a procession
        of courtesy-gestures, in turn:
                ran the tap over the back
Of her hand until it was cool,
        turned it off, off on
                to give me the clearest
Available; I thanked her
        with my best smile, to which
                she replied 'Have you
A pension-book? if you have,
        go to the British Legion,
                they will give you a free
Meal . . .' I smiled and said
        I would do this in
                a couple of years, and smiled
With more care and repeated thanks
        keeping my voice slightly
                high and elderly
Which it was anyway though I did not quite
        have the pension-book, not quite;
                smiling we parted,
She like a white officer, and I had
                contacted a friendship

Of those who have grown old
        and offer me a glass
                from the elder house of waters
With a ceremony that was private and kindly meant,
        drawing the water, in white, as if
                she had been and was still
In service in a great house
        Among the waters;
                the friendship of those
Who learn to grow old
        where our rooms are readying,
                old as waters.

THE CHESHIRE SMILE

Nudity: screwing
        through a wonderful house
                that begins unfurnished;
As many pilchards in the bay
        as if the water were boiling;
                the white birds that lounge
About the precipices
        waiting the moment;
                she brought me likewise
Into a large place;
        she delivered me because
                she delighted in me;
By virtue of her large gown
        she wrapped me round and round
                in the world, and there was
That pierceable forge of water,
        that bumping spring.
                        And there are certain rains
That come from a higher heaven;
        the valleys grow chymical
In twilight.
        He picked up a minute pebble, it was rock-
                crystal carved into a skull,
He turned it round and round
        against the light, the smile
                appearing and disappearing
Through the facial contours and the cranium
        like the Cheshire Cat's;
                she turned the evening round him
Likewise, her smile
        appearing, disappearing.

THE VERDURER

The verderer records
           the woodsound in his notebook
                      to study the tree's pulses
Indoors. As he returns
           he passes under the wild pines
                      wracked by their anguish
To great size.
           These trees are avatars
                      of the books on his shelves,
The foliage blowing open
           blowing shut –
                      he knows their titles,
Scotch Pine. Crackwillow,
           Alder,
                      and reads their green;
The library is an avatar
           of the forest, with each book
                      a haunted corner
Until he closes
           the wooden covers
                      'When in such an embrace
Your nerves are shaken as leaves,
           enter this shaking'
                      he leaves
This book or forest
           wide open on the wooden table
                      for its good advice.

CORNWALL MUD

Look, here in the mud
             is a small Cornwall,
                        deeply ridged,
The claypuddle footprint
             in the drying wind.
                        This puddle dries
With the globe of the sun
             writing on it, it dries
                        to the Moon,
And to Venus ascending;
             Saturn, Mars
                        parch it likewise:
It is the wind of purposes
             or ghost
                        leaves its wingbeats
In these puddles; you can play back
             these influences
                        with this blossoming stick,
As if a small Eve
             struggled to pull her Adam
                        out of the sticky matrix,
Reading the wingbeats like Genesis.

LAWN SPRINKLER AND LIGHTHOUSE

(at the Lizard)

A water-sprinkler seen in the seaward meadow,
        a complex ghost-pulse
                seen, low in the meadow
By lighthouse-beam:
        a dew machine,
                a complex ghost-pulse
Beaten out by the beam
        sweeping the meadow
                a screen of mist against which
The lighthouse beam pumps carousel,
        the screen pulsing in itself,
                and the beam swinging across,
The cycle of each drawing
        together, and drawing apart:
                the sprinkler's almost invisible
Dewy head bowing to the great beam,
        white shadow of the spray
                of the water-ghost vanishing
And appearing again
        in a new place,
                pacing out its ghost-circle
Under the orbit of the lighthouse,
        in the beam, white, faint
                like faint chalk
On a dusky board, in the shadow
        of the whirling beam, felloe
                whirling round its nub
Above; below the spray beating in
        several soft arcs of a shining house traced
                under the lighthouse,

And with a turn of the clouds
        the full moon with its clouds
                full of its light.

THE GOOD OLD WOMAN

(Trerice)

Drawn in fine lines
             in many pastel shades
                          a complex wall-housemap
Declaring multiplex rooms, long galleries
             shining staircases, etc.; I
                          try to find on the map
The window I am standing at; it is called
             Sea Room but what I see
                          is a gravel drive with yews
Where should hover the sea,
             blue and bright:
                          where does this house
Hide its ocean? shall I walk out
             behind this closet door
                          behind this stair down
Lighted with invisible torches, walk
             out undersea over the sandy bottom
                          under the phosphor
God-masks of the sea-bass?
             An old woman has parked
                          her white car on the gravel
An off-white dented Mini, and as the engine
             revs, the car
Moves out slowly like a dimpled moon
             shedding its full beams in low gear
                          tugging the yew walk
And driveway away with her, like a map
             leaving the sea
To me out of the *Sea-Room* window.

SEEDING THE ANCIENT PINE

The scaly wooden cone having
        rested so many years
                on my table cut from pine
One morning without
        warning with a rustle
                let out a shoal of seeds
Like winged heads of Hermes
        feathery-light, dry and dead
                or sleeping with wooden lids;
I took the handful to Killigrew Gardens
        to broadcast then on the laurel-shadowed air,
                threw them into the light breeze –
How they wisping spun like pinewood propellers
        spinning in a flock
Of pinwheels pinewheels that were wooden birds
        that were pine-trees, spinning:
                fallen out of their ancient cone
With a latter-day click, like
        one tock of an old clock.

LIMESTONE CAT

for N.R.

I

I throw a pebble in the lake
        I see the shape
                of a sitting cat
In the moment it leaves
        my hand, enthroned cat
                it breaks the roof
Of the lake, the one pebble
        fills the surface
                with its shape:
The vibrating depths
        organise themselves
                into that shape –
In the lake's dark
        the stone cat comes
                to life, prowling
Like a night-companion. The mass
        of waters forms itself
                round the small host
Which enters the church of waters
        and alters them, each ripple
                is aroused in a purr-shape,
Which touches the lake's rafters,
        in invisible chanting.

I search the shore for another cat
            to throw after the first
                        and find only
Buddha-stones – I throw
            Buddha in a pebble and again
                        the whole lake
Reorganises itself, something calmer
            sits down in its centre, but the cat-ripples
                        prowl round
The seated sage who ripples
            in his own time,
                        Buddha and cat who
Seeks his lap
            through the whole lake,
                        cat and Buddha –
The same water in different
            sequences, cat prowls
                        like a walking-master
Who can with gold discs
            see in the lake-dark,
                        Buddha sits.

III

I find a pebble
            like a child sleeping
                        a stone baby curled
Up into itself; if I throw it back
            into the cradle of waters
                        it will wake up the cat,

Then the Buddha, then itself
                in child-signatures, wet echoes,
                                as it rearranges the water,
Anything, it depicts
                anything:
                                Catlake, Buddhawater,
Sleepingchildlake;
                I threw a cat-pebble in
                                to alter the religion
To alter the water, like a woman
                pinning a cameo to her collar;
                                the folds of her dress,
The coiler, fall
                into a new pattern,
                                of its own accord,
Shaped by everything.

MAKING THE BED

The bedclothes were a long twin-dress:
The one dress between two.

Keeping only her own face and breasts
She took the form of a salmon in bed.

The place where poetry was revealed
Was always on the brink of water.

She got out of bed
Like plucking her rootlets free.

By lying down in the crisp linen
The mirror you open to in the dreams,

The door you open in the cool earth
By lying your self down in the mirror-stuff:

Immediately like a white cat at its milk
Lapping in it.

HUGE OLD

(from the Welsh Virgil Caverns)

These are the huge old
         may trees so full of flowers
                they seem already woven into gardens
On Hay Bluff
        the air like childhood air:
              on the Pilgrim mountains
Silkier.
        Trees pour ghost
              from tree to tree;
The torrents of scent
        splash into flowers, the flowers
              splash back again into scent;
Each small flower blows
        sweet smell like a swirling fanfare:
              the health of it
Is like low thunder, the great
        escarpment bending forward
              with a pressure of silence;
The silence is scented even in the core
        of the wind-shadow.

THE FLYING ACE

The Flying Ace, the Ace of Birds,
That perfect soul-bird, the owl, the werewoman,
The perfect soul-woman;

The mask zooms under the trees
And hangs itself up, watching
Through 270 degrees, making uterus-face.

It sees by wisdom-light, its own
Hot body-lamp, its stare means
Truthfulness, inside the head
Is folded a purple garment, showing
At the pupils, like the night.

Mice, trampled in this gut
To a bony wafer of fur.

As the magnetism of wisdom surrounds it
You must break the monopoly:
Bring a particle of light from elsewhere,
A smaller bird humming
Into our spectrum . . .

As for that Ace,
The eyes are always clean
From nictitation, like a priest's eyes,
Polishing its own eyeballs constantly
To enlarge intensely
The sphere of intelligible dark.

THE COMFORTERS

Gullet Quarry and Clatters Cave
        at Malvern
                look as they sound;
There are dykes called 'Elvans'
        filled and shining
                with quartz porphyry;
A rock from Derbyshire
        composed entirely
                of flies' wings; it is bats
That strip the small flies of their wings
        and transform them
                into a kind of fairy coprolite;
Wings everwhere!
        and that mountain presence
                brings forth all jades
And sulphurs crusted in scales
        on which the dragonflies settle
                in their jade wings;
It is everywhere
        the winged Friends in stone
                who do not change
Their perfume, she
        is the same presence
                everywhere (and the heart-pulses
Of the water-scent; water
        dropping on stone
                illuminating it,
Wearing it away.)

A TEAM OF GLAZIERS

The great bay window
        glittered like the compound eye
                of a giant Northern insect,
The frosty compound eye.
        A woman changes
             her maternity clothes,
The forest flowers
        as all the women change
             their maternity dresses
Garments billowing
        as if we rode
             inside a fluttering mothbody;
He will look so much like his father
        he will be called Gordon's little ghost
             the child as dowser
Somersaults in the bay-window belly
        as she passes over the blind springs,
             turns round in the belly,
Revolving homestead; a team of glaziers
        refurbishes the southern window,
             the house with its cascade
Of windows, glitters with the sunrise,
             the vast fractured sandgrain,
The mesmeric presence of a pebble
        that by fractal repeats the coast-line,
             it is both large and small at once,
I lift it, I lift the look
        of ten thousand tons,
             I rattle the cliffs in my hand.

SLEEPERS' BEACH

(Perranporth)

Echoes of an Atlantic storm
        gentled by the distance travelled
             mingling with the echoes
Re-echoing off the dark cliffs:
        they break in the longsand
             like the day's sleepiness;
Somebody is dreaming this beach
        with the vibrant 'tubes' rolled in
             in their musical order,
The invisible wings of this dreamer
        wafting sleep-breeze
             that slides over the sandhills
Where a ruined oratory hides
        whose stones wear away
             into sleepy sand
Full of balsam; now the stout
        and lively rain
             conjures over the dry sand
Immense water-shadings which
        project a chill; the already
             glass-wet beach stretches away
To the headland we call
        Skull Island and the clouds
             are white supersurf above
Excelling the surfer's surf,
        who wear in the white water
             dark sea-tadpole-suits,

And the red flag goes up
  to mark the perilous abysses
      that seek to come ashore.

BUZZ

I feared the miracle
        of the next day's waking,
                my bed was jammed against the wall
On my right, there was wallpaper
        with a vibratory pattern I forget,
                it went 3D and on the
Other side was a sinister organist
        playing his metals: it is now
                the organs on my right side
That are vulnerable, groin and pancreas.
        I wanted mental marvels
                from simple sleeping pills
And caffeine tablets,
        got some from laburnum seeds,
                safe when dried.
I fixed a little box with a buzzer in it
        on my bicycle-front to ride to school with,
                to signify I was being charged up
Or electrified by the journey, batterybuzzer;
        the bicycle bell was for emergencies
                that would break the trance,
Like the navigator natives on Darwin,
        a little flap of cloth would recharge
                the whole person's perceptions:
I did this by buttoning and unbuttoning
        my shirt as I rode; it was rare
                and to be remarked upon
To see an open shirt
        on the way to Esher;
                I am still the boy riding there
Or as far as Guildford
        among the buzzing, the coloured
                and tactile images. Once

I stopped at a cinema on the way:
    a woman in ample Victorian dress
        slipped and fell into a garden pond
In which she sat enraged, her beige skirt
    struck shit-colour instantly,
        with a shine –
What a vision! even women could get
    sexy-wet, especially women; Jesus
        offered living water to the women
At her well, but these were cunni-waters
    and her own element and familiar.
        Come and be well! my skin
Was transparent as water
    with that vision of exterior cunt.
        She offered her pond,
The woman in the flowing shirts,
    and in the Song, the woman lover
        is a fountain of living waters.
I could not send these visions away,
    not for long anyway,
        they were an ultimate for me.
The Sin is not the visions,
    but is quenching the visions:
        quench not the Spirit (1, Th. 5.19);
I knew something too of
    the dry water of the alchemists
        it was the vibratory
And streaming atmosphere my mother
    could make in bed, and she was wise
        with the bouquet of her skin,
Her dreaming breath, and mine.
    How that woman of the pond
        glittered in her new clothes;
What is that dream
    you are having this instant;

                   how her jet necklaces shine
Like stars that are dark
         and bright at once;
                  out of her belly
Living water, water
         that will not be quenched.

THE DARK BELL

The galleons of ocean
   pass overhead,
     the mist comes down
And you are immediately at sea,
   the air becomes silly,
     approaching thunder
Rings its changes
   and everybody's breath-rhythm changes;
     short pulses of benign water,
Then larger, sleepier drops,
   the whole situation
     lies fallow
In long deep drops
   of heavier rain,
     the entire coast alters
But she was well-clitorised
   for the fourth time
     that Sunday;
The bell did it,
   the great bell of Long Rock:
     'I call the living,
I mourn the dead,
   I break the thunder,'
     says the monster;
For the fourth time this Sunday
   the bell broke the thunder,
     the penis, clitoris,
And the vagina
   have entered this world
     from higher regions,

For the fourth time this Sunday
                    giving themselves
                                        to the dark garden,
The other church;
                    looked out, thought
                                        it was a ship
Tending to anchor;
                    then the bell struck –
                                        it was a long rock
With foam up to the gunwhales
                    sending out soundless pulses
                                        breaking the thunder
Creating the silence
                    for the fourth time that Sunday

II

As the lake and the cloud
                    came close
                                        they were like two
Electrical smooth plates,
                    the tension between them
                                        created a palpable
Hush, an emission
                    of hush; the lake
                                        was so smooth now
It looked as if the whole
                    thundercloud had been dropped
                                        into it; she had
Just come to the stable door
                    when she was suddenly
                                        delivered of her child
Without effort, the lake
                    was so smooth, and the rain without effort

began to deliver itself,
And a county of rain fell
like a white forest
with blowing in it
Rain-horses
coursing without effort;
mother and child
From the stable doorway waved back
to the faint thunder like hooves
inexhaustably passing overhead.

MONETA CLOCK

I

From the top of the stairs
        comes the slow salaaming tick
                of a very old clock
In a mahogany case –
        time told in the forest shade
                bringing its tall shadow indoors,
Time standing in still timber;
        coffin-clock stands on the stairs.

II

There are nervy clouds,
        fast-moving,
                high up:
Succeeded by grumbling
        and bumptious thunderclouds;
                a furnace roars back at them
Like an enraged disowned ancestor
        in the basement
                who is carnivorous.
She drives along
        under the moon
                in its shell of ice,
A pallid round rainbow
        or ice-halo
                in ivory colours:
Some of it cracks
        into a hailstorm
                that patters on

Her white car
            like the sounds
                        of broken glass
Falling on white armour.
                  The clouds are low
                              grazing on the electricity
Budding out of the floodwater –
            they won't shift,
                        they seal-in the creek
Creating a thunder
            which is the ponderous
                        tick-tock subsonic
Of their champing,
            a sound that quickly becomes
                        an oppressive emotion:
One immense muffling fleece
            packing out the valleys:
                        that is how
The clouds graze here.
I consult the lady Doctor
            for my delusions as above,
                        I become aware as I speak
Of the nectar-she, who
            continually secretes night and day
                        from herself; her
Deeply-sloping flower,
            her living medicine,
                        her extra qualification.
My rashes itch like the weather of my skin:
            'Hold on!' she counsels –
                        then the rain loosens
And the misty flocks depart
            into and through the rushing streams:
                        now I can see

The Doctor clearly in her white coat
        and she smiles,
                her nectar crackles underneath
Like land-electricity, grazing ghosts,
        she wears it like a dazzling holly-bush.

DENTIST-CONJURERS

The dentist-conjurers,
             initiates into the white robes;
                          because of all their signs –
The sharp white coats,
             the surgical smiles and smells,
                          the subtle tools that clink
Into sonorous dishes,
             the fountain of circular water
                          you spit into, and that the tooth
Is gone, only a footprint remains,
             and the bite gone –
                          you allow them into your mouth
With their condom fingers.
             Time is altered, the teeth
                          enlarged into mountain ranges;
A rubber touch to the lip
             it strolls on the edge
                          of cruelty, the deep
Black torture-chairs
             their cushioned comfort
                          awaiting pain, that see-saw
And swing on the same touch,
             a small sharp pain
                          into the gum secures
Against a fully-developed pain
             in the darkness like a magician's hat
                          turned inside-out
That is your mouth in which
             wispy shadow-rabbit shapes are
                          reflected from the instruments
And their rubbery touch,
             and then a rending, profoundly
                          unfelt though it might be

That the anaesthetic breaks
                  and cancels, atrocious pain,
                                  the brink that is everywhere
But not here, not in this mouth
                  which is a shadow-play,
                                  a dreaming-place of
Snapping rafters, shattered stone;
                  It is my pain but feels like another's hurt,
                                  borrowed calm, and I walk
Away with one lip caught up painless
                  in a snarling invisible hook
                                  with a ferocious lisp
But strengthened with fresh biting power
                  in a perfect gummy shell
                                  eating as an oyster eats,
Flap flap the
                  digestible pap now rules
                                  O.K.?
Where does the pain go?
                  everywhere but in this room
                                  of bright light
And comfortable deep torture chairs.

UNDER TAKER

The gold foil lettering,
             In pine, in elm-panelled rooms,
                          the colloquy of prices;
On entry from the common street
             the environment alters
                          since you are entering
The ghost-train
             the first class, elm-panelled
                          African snakewood salon.
A man with a sombre beard,
             a pleasant though grave expression,
                          approaches like somebody
Who has seen everything.
             he will discuss everything
                          in his parlour
Where a parley is laid in account
             with a third party, called dead.
                          You would not have thought
That such matters could be discussed
             in that lot or plot
Between the house-agent's and the grocer's;
                          they are undertakers
People who under-stand, stand up
                          under this wax-polished portal
In whose cellars cosmetics are confected
             agreeable to the eye
                          where the deceased
Will finish her struggle as a waxwork
             in the small broken parlours
                          of rotting elm and deceased pine
Dressed as La Traviata, leaving
             a coffin-shaped doorway in the mourner,
                          who is executing dead wishes

That fill up the parlour
             with a colloquy as an anaesthetic
                          that in the circumstances
Is agreeable; here is somebody
             to talk death with when most
                          avoid it, and prices
Are reachable. There are many mansions
             broken in this soil;
                          she must have a good send-off,
This is the first-class station
             gleaming with wax polish
                          and we walk up and down
The platform discussing death
             while the train waits
                          for the right moment
To steam off with shivering plumes;
             it is the funeral train – be careful
                          to get off before it leaves;
Its frigid corridors are full
             of daffodils, so bright, the sun
                          shines underground; the light
Must come from somewhere
             in this black.

A WALK BY THE HELSTON PONDS

A walk by the Helston Ponds
   she remarks how from
     the nooks of an oak
The primrose flowers begin to glow
   with an incipient sunshine
     just before the sun itself
Comes out:
   you look up and the clouds
    are thinning –
There's no sun yet
   yet the primroses shine
    as if lit from below;
So sun shines on earth
   before it shines in heaven
    and shines upwards:
'For heavene myghte nought holden it
   it was so hevy of hym-self'
     I see a greenlad sapling
Step out of the hedgerow
   with broadleaf shoulders pause
    in a sunbeam, a small quickset
Springs like a human kiss
   and the ponds are heavy with sunlight
    (We read in this morning's news
That the Queen had moved the Crown Jewels
   to a new display in the Tower
    where they are lit from below.)

Working in a little tent
              the Healers, three of them,
                            under the cast-iron rafters of the echoing
Exhibition hall;
              my daughter Z
                            went into them
And emerged shining
              like Moses off the Mount,
                            would never tell me
What happened in the
              off-white tabernacle
                            that shone her up so;
I knew it was supposed to be not touch,
              but meridians of wildfire, of bio-energy
                            speeding over the skin like a
Shunting yard at night.
                            I approached the Chief Clairvoyant:
                            she took one look at me,
This old lady and said:
              'You're a Glory-Boy. What do you want
                            of us, Glory-Boy . . .'
I was taken aback. Was it really
              or entirely that I wanted
                            Own Glory, or was it truly
To extend spirit into body
              and body to spirit. As she berated me
                            I saw her clairvoyance
By my own:
              a great butterfly or moth has fastened
                            itself to her brow
At the 'third eye', and its wings were
              beating over her forehead,
                            as if to fly.

The interior beautiful
        as the hair of a Magdelen,
                an interior mystery,
The angel with owl's wings;
        the monkey perched on the lectern
                is the first to notice
The fatherlight shot down
        from the upper cabinet,
                bats and vampires
In friezes building up the groining
        the nave at right angles
                existing for that moment,
The horned devils
        watering the trefoils,
                basil, foxglove, belladonna,
With the black lily in the obsidian vase:
        herbs for a clear womb;
                both Father and batangel
Making figthumbs;
        a menstrual mandala in stained glass
                refracting the Father's rays
From the upper gallery –
        rays pouring from his active finger
                the ovum rotting into gold light
And a new testament,
        the Father's high angel attending on him
                with butterfly wings
Releasing in-sense in wing pulses,
        the roses on the Virgin's
                rose-robes opening to the fingerlight,
Holding the half-dark sphere in the palm
        of his hand, all
                shall be well in the shadows of her

Shining cape, Thoth reading a litany
                in many voices from his lectern
                            made of monkey-wood and goathorn.

ELECTRICITIES OF THE CAT

A catspaw, a little brainstorm,
    a kind of blip in the air,
        the cat an electrical fit, black spark
Chasing birds, flashing
    voltage fangs;
        household objects are lost
Temporarily when the cat strikes or
    catercrawls like a swift slug;
        thunder appears first on earth
As small black cat bodies,
    thunder-cat, cat-thunder
        that spins the cat
In claws of lightning
    that slash the trees,
        strip to the coracle;
Then there are the bolts of remembering
    after the rain has fallen
        and we walk under the spent storms
In winged easystretch shoulderblades
    that beat to touch the underceiling
        of residual thunder
Muttering in subsonics
    the whole purr of the world (Falmouth twinned
        with a Chinese village; so back here
We write not so much about
    clouds, rain, cats and thunder
        as by means of them).

The satisfaction
   of the king's oil,
      the black oil
Of the tree's engine,
   dipping one's hand
      into the engine-oil
Of everything;
   with your ear to the bark
      hear the all-creaking
Of the balsam-press
   as if grapes were being trod;
      the corpus rotundum
Or acorn
   built the tree about itself
      as a stronghold;
The tree wills that anything
   under its great branches
      must shine with balsam
Darkly;
   one touches this balsam and sticks,
      becomes the infant
Of the tree anointed
   with the oil of coronation
      from the tree's crown;
There is an electrical timber –
   balsam ascending;
      and a balsam of foliage
Sinking with fragrance;
   and there is the mudlark,
      uniting myself
With the all-balsam
   from the under-forest,

                              robed in the forest,
          Greeted by the forest,
                    created by the forest.

THE AVENUE

I

The gigantic labours
                rise on either hand
                        of the gardeners,
But truly they didn't raise
                a finger, to ensoul the trees,
                        the tree-avenues
Like gods visiting
                in their green temples;
                        the gardeners' only task
Being to provide fertile habitations
                as for gods that rise of themselves
                        and breathe themselves green;
What are they made of? The trees on either hand
                rise like mansions
                        opening and closing
Green doors and shutters,
                water and air having elected
                        to become timber
Tabernacles, where they themselves shall dwell.
                The cabinets of the seed open wide
                        and futher avenues
March out, throwing their feeding
                green doors wide open
                        on every side.

II

The old people on the lawn
                feed on the sun, winter

after winter their woodgrain
Wrinkles deepen, they too
will become water, wind
and wood; they become
Gardeners, without having
to lift a finger.

APPRENTICE

My father at the bonfire
        in the garden, under the great
                sycamore tree near the laburnum
Into which I climbed
        to poison myself with
                its green fruit, black fruit;
The tree of a knowledge
        that peeled scales
                from my eyes –
Illumination and sickness
        in the tiny studs;
                my father demonstrating
The unreeling snake
        he had made visible in the wind,
                demonstrating to me the demons
And daemons of the smoke in the garden
        polished up by the perilous laburnum;
                demonstration of the horses
Of fire stampeding in their smoky stables,
        the doors of smoke opening and slamming
                on the lighted interiors;
The great magician working
        and the sorcerer's apprentice working
                clapping the planks together
To lift into the blaze the juicy boughs;
        his cacky or khaki shirt opening and closing
                in the heat
Spiritual earth of soldier's shirt; his
        invisible beard and robes
                tinctured into visibility
By the laburnum's permission
        showing me the world that came
                on the wind that was him;

(My mother conducted me
        between the surfing of the poplars
                telling her tales of them
Simply of themselves on the wind, to and fro
        exchanging stories of gentle monsters,
                favourable green phantom fountains.)
My father rushed the wind
        turning the solid wood to fluid smoke
                that travelled over the world
Crying out laburnum! from
        the clouds where I can see to this day
                his white merlin shadows in the clouds,
And he tends his bonfire
        that removes still
                innumerable further scales from
My apprentice eyes.